Arnold
Circus
Stool,
Martino
Gamper

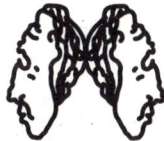

Arnold Circus Stool, Martino Gamper
First edition published in 2022 by Dent-De-Leone
Editors: åbäke, Gemma Holt, Martino Gamper and Sarah Simpkin
Writers: Martino Gamper, Robin Hatton-Gore (originally
published in 2018), Alex Klein, Michael Marriott, Cornelia
Parker (originally published in *Financial Times* Magazine
24/04/2015), Anna Salaman and Rainer Spehl

Design: åbäke
Photographers:
åbäke (16, 21, 23, 26–27, 29, 41, 68, 76–77, 87)
Courtesy Carnegie Museum of Art © Alex Klein (35)
Courtesy ICA Philadelphia (36–37)
Courtesy Pinacoteca Giovanni e Marella Agnelli
© Andrea Guermani (73)
Courtesy Nilufar Gallery © Andrea Riboni (46–47 [stools], 52–53)
Courtesy MUDAM © Andres Lejona (69)
Angus Mill (cover, 42–47, 54–57, 60, 79–80, 91–93, 96)
Anna Arca (2–3, 50–51, 68, 70)
Bishopsgate Institute archive *The Municipal Journal* 1900 (6)
Courtesy Nilufar Gallery © Daniele Iodice (58–59)
Courtesy Galleria Franco Noero (48–49, 62, 78)
Courtesy *British Art Show* 8, Leeds Art Gallery
© Jerry Hardman-Jones (72)
Courtesy Hamburg Kunstverein (46–47)
London Metropolitan Archives, City of London (11)
Courtesy Institute of Contemporary Arts © Marcus Leith (71)
Mario Ciampi, first published in *Italian Designers at Home*, 2006 (25)
Martino Gamper Studio (31–32, 51, 61, 63–65, 81–82)
Matylda Krzykowski (39, 95)
Courtesy Peter Pilotto (59, 66–67)
Courtesy Project Dublin (74–75)

Photographs in this publication document or aestheticise the
possible uses for the stools. We trust your judgement to not
consider this publication as a manual, but simply the life of an
object from its conception through its transformations by Martino
Gamper. Be inspired, but don't follow blindly. It is telling of our
times we even have to print this. In short and as a practical
example, if you need to drill holes in a wall, we recommend
the using the proper tools, training and wearing shoes.

THE MUNICIPAL JOURNAL.

ESTABLISHED AS "LONDON."

No. 370.—Vol. IX.   MARCH 2, 1900.

Municipal Housing in London.

Prince and Princess of Wales open the L.C.C. Dwellings in Bethnal Green to-morrow. From Slums to Model Dwellings.—Full Descriptions of the Scheme.

THE Prince and Princess of Wales visit Bethnal-green to-morrow to formally declare open the last of the buildings erected in the Boundary-street area. We publish in the follow-ing pages a complete description of this great clearance and housing scheme. We trace the transformation of the fifteen acres of slumland from the beginning of the investigation to the completion of the model colony of municipal dwellings. It is the biggest work of the kind ever undertaken by any municipal authority, and well merits the prominence which it will receive from the Royal visit.

VIEW OF BOUNDARY STREET BUILDINGS SHOWING GARDEN MOUND.

My London: Arnold Circus
Cornelia Parker, 2015

I first stumbled across Arnold Circus and the Boundary Estate in 1993, lost en route to the opening of Tracey Emin and Sarah Lucas's shop in nearby Redchurch Street, where they sold their first artworks. The area then seemed thrillingly scary and run down, with barely lit streets and towering, grimy red-brick tenements. It felt more reminiscent of 1960s Glasgow or Berlin than London. Later that evening, my friends and I bought carry-out beers from an Irish pub, The Dolphin (now chic hardware shop, Labour and Wait). In the bar a few very drunk locals slouching on dilapidated sofas peered at us through the smoke. A disembodied slurred voice told us to serve ourselves, take bottles from the bar and leave the money in a jar, as it seemed no one was sober enough to serve us. When we passed the pub again in the early hours, they were still in there singing, a muffled lock-in with the curtains drawn. There began my long and continuing love affair with the area.

At the time I lived in Leytonstone, part of a community of artists in short-term housing. A year later, in 1994, my house was knocked down for the long-threatened M11 link road (remember Swampy?), and we were forced to move on, good friends scattered to the four winds. Answering the call of the inner city, I moved to Shoreditch and stayed for the next 20 years, living at three different addresses a few metres apart. With only enough deposit to get a mortgage for £35,000, I bought a former council flat in Old Nichol Street. The mortgage was very hard to obtain as valuers told me no one in their right mind would want to live there. Granted the flat had its drawbacks. Two drug-addled teenage boys on the floor below me played music so loud every plate and cup jumped, and the flat above seemed to be operating as a sweatshop. It was like being trapped in a noise sandwich. After a couple of years of frayed nerves, but reluctant to leave the area, I sold up and moved into a rented attic flat next door on Arnold Circus.

In the centre of the Circus is a bandstand built on top of a raised mound, made of rubble from the levelling of London's most notorious Victorian slum. The Old Nichol was a squalid, densely populated hell's kitchen, made famous by Arthur Morrison's 1896 novel *A Child of the Jago*. The infamous warren of streets, full of disease, prostitutes and thieves was cleared in the 1890s to make way for the Boundary Estate, the first council housing in Britain. The listed Arts and Crafts estate is made up of highly individual red- and yellow-brick buildings variegated with the occasional stripe. Streets lined with these imposing tenements fan out from the Circus, softened by the lofty London plane trees. The streets have beautiful-sounding names like Navarre, Ligonier, Montclare, Camlet and Palissy.

From my attic window I could witness the drug traffic that used to monopolise the bandstand. Groups of Bangladeshi youths would gather and disperse, occasionally getting into skirmishes with local Indian gangs. It was their turf, none of the other locals dared to venture up there. The slopes of the mound were overgrown with shrubs perfect for hiding illicit activities. More recently, the bandstand has been reclaimed and refurbished by The Friends of Arnold Circus, who organise spontaneous music events, summer fairs and kids' races around the Circus, spearheaded by the wonderful Leila McAllister, whose Leila's Café and Deli was a brave pioneer in what was a culinary wilderness.

Back then, in the 1990s, the beautifully named streets were the place to dump stolen cars. You could tell if a vehicle was abandoned as it would be quickly dismembered, losing its tyres one by one until it was picked clean by invisible lions. If anyone was parked anywhere near they knew to move their car, as inevitably the wreck would be torched that night. Nowadays the streets are populated with Lamborghinis and Porsches with their car alarms going off intermittently, their drivers happily ensconced in clubs like nearby Shoreditch House or in Conran's Albion bistro. London taxi drivers often drew a blank at my address. They acted as if they were entering the Bermuda Triangle. The ones who did know it were inevitably those brought up on the estate itself, having long since decamped to the leafy suburbs of Chingford and Woodford. They would regale me with stories of their childhood, of mothers and grandmothers dancing on the bandstand on Sundays, and welcomed the excuse to visit Syd's, a famous cabbies' tea stand 100m away on Calvert Avenue, open five days a week since 1919.

On the southeast corner of Arnold Circus is the old Rochelle School. It was snapped up by a property developer in the mid-80s and lay fallow for years (acquiring considerable value), during which time it was squatted by travellers. That meant being woken in the middle of the night by caravans arriving and departing. Someone there was keeping peacocks, their shrill cries adding drama to the nightscape. Now it is home to the A Foundation, a complex of artist studios, a gallery and the offices of Frieze Art magazine. Hidden behind the wall of the school, housed in a metal shed, is the sublime Rochelle Canteen, a lunchtime restaurant run by chef Margot Henderson and Melanie Arnold. Serving new British cuisine, it is place of pilgrimage for those in the know. The Canteen was where I celebrated my 50th birthday on a very hot day one July.

When I moved again, it was back to Old Nichol Street, this time buying a small Victorian warehouse which served as both as studio and home for me, my husband and daughter for 15 years.

Shoreditch has been gradually colonised by artists, designers and architects, attracted by low property prices and dilapidated commercial spaces. Like in every major city, gentrification inevitably follows. The big-boy developers move in, rents and property prices shoot up and the artists move on. A couple of years ago we moved to a house in North London close to a good state school. We still love visiting the neighbourhood, usually on Sunday, when a short walk north from the Circus takes us to Columbia Road Flower Market (for our exotic plant needs) or a short walk south takes us to Brick Lane Market (for everything else).

The Arnold Circus in 1900

The Bandstand
Robin Hatton-Gore, 2018

The eight-sided bandstand at Arnold Circus has been a treasured landmark at the centre of the historic Boundary Estate for over a century. The only constant hereabouts is change and the bandstand has witnessed its fair share of changes.

There is an unusual energy in this location that is perhaps preternatural and the raised mound has generated apocryphal tales of ancient myth, suggesting it is on a ley line connected to St Martin-in-the-Fields. Other local legends stem from an earlier site called Friars' Mount nearby, where "a set of fellows lived in laziness and luxury." A vivid but scurrilous account by the anti-Papist author, George Borrows, in his 1874 *Gypsy Dictionary* fancifully attributes the name Friars' Mount to a former friary. It is more likely derived from a John Fryer, who "farmed the field around a small hillock on Mount Street" in the 1720s. This mound, in even earlier times, may have formed part of a military rampart — a link in "a chain of twenty-three fortifications" — which Parliamentarians used to defend London against Royalist forces in the English Civil War.

Yet the truth is that the mound is of more recent origin, and the historical reality is more interesting than the myth. The Housing of the Working Classes Act of

1890 heralded the dismantling of the Old Nichol, the notorious rookery which stood here before. Arthur Morrison wrote a fictional account of the Old Nichol in 1896 entitled, *A Child of the Jago*. He derived 'the Jago' from the name of Rev Osborne Jay, an adherent of the Muscular Christianity movement, who ran a boxing gym below his Church of Holy Trinity. Morrison had first been invited to the Old Nichol by Rev Jay, and the novel was published only after the ramshackle structures of this most scandalous of slums had been razed.

In 1897, *The British Architect* journal reported: "The London County Council for some years past has been devoting the energies of their staff to the preparation of a grand scheme for the rehousing of the working classes. A site near Shoreditch Church was selected for this purpose, and the Boundary Street Working Class Housing Dwellings are well worth visiting now... the plan is that of a great circus, in the middle of which, on an elevated plateau there is to be a bandstand."

In 1889, Owen Fleming became the leader of the London County Council's (LCC) new 'Housing of the Working Classes' branch, a group of young, progressive architects tasked with the creation of a pioneering collection of buildings to raise the standard of housing for labourers and artisans in one of the poorest districts of the East End. This was to be the very first council housing estate. Social housing had existed previously, funded by charity, but the Boundary was the first financed by the taxpayer. Thomas Blashill, the LCC's Superintendent Architect, entrusted this group of architects — who were inspired by the Arts and Crafts movement — to create 23 domestic buildings, each subtly different.

In an inspired move, the architects rejected an already-approved grid for the scheme. Fleming fought "to be allowed to build the central raised garden with its bandstand, around which he had imagined the local courting couples strolling on a summer's evening while the band played." Seven streets radiated from the unifying hub of Arnold Circus like the spokes of a wheel. The architectural diversity of the buildings included details and features that were in contrast to the uniformity of style which had formerly marked the housing of the poor.

The rubble displaced in digging out the foundations was piled up to become Boundary Gardens, a fact confirmed by Museum of London Archaeology when they excavated in 2012 and discovered artefacts belonging to the former residents of the Old Nichol.

On the Boundary Estate, street names derive from the towns of Huguenot immigrants: Rochelle, Navarre and Montclare. Arnold Circus itself is named after Sir Arthur Arnold, a Liberal and chairman of the

London County Council. The surrounding buildings are named after towns along the Thames: Cookham, Chertsey and Henley. The *Architectural Association Journal* said: "the central garden... is more than a piece of pattern-making by the architects, it is a strong unifying factor which does much to make of the scheme a community rather than a collection of model dwellings."

Friends of Arnold Circus: The Early Days
Anna Salaman, Board member, Friends of Arnold Circus 2004–2009

A vision grew out of that first public meeting in 2004, of a place that would be safe for all, be attractive, have entertainment at certain points, encourage community participation, be a place to look at art, to take part in celebrations or just a place to sit quietly and be refreshed.

Naseem Khan, 2005
Friends of Arnold Circus Chair

It seems hard to believe now, but when the Friends of Arnold Circus was formed in 2004, the bandstand and its surrounds were in a state of disrepair, overgrown and neglected. Few people ventured up to the space. In fact, most of the local residents deemed it to be unsafe, poorly lit, and unhygienic. There were no benches, no flowers, some of the iron railings were broken or missing, and the Victorian bandstand itself was unstable and unappealing.

It is quite remarkable that the Friends of Arnold Circus turned around the space so quickly. Herculean levels of voluntary work both behind and in front of the scenes brought about this transformation. At the helm was Naseem Khan OBE, the undisputed tour de force of the movement. Leila McAlister was the leading voice of passion and vision combined, and other residents provided time, support and valued skills. I was Vice-Chair of the Board of Trustees, securing the charitable status for the organisation and taking the lead in membership and fundraising. I remember putting together the first mailing list consisting of 25 names; three years later, it numbered over 400.

Operating at full pelt, the organisation ran six open events in the financial year 2005–06, attracting between 100 and 1000 people to each. These events combined the old with the new, in recognition of the heritage that continues to form such an integral part of the bandstand's iconography, and of its resurgence to fulfil a vital, valid role for the contemporary communities that lived around it. For that year, the events included a brass band performance replete with deck chairs, tea and cake, and a 'sharing picnic' with donkey rides, a communal 100-lap cycling event around the Circus, live music and storytelling. There was a Carrom event, with the resident Bangladeshi community and uninitiated newcomers together playing the popular South Asian board game, and the memorable 'Harmonize' — a magical evening of music from different cultures and genres. In 2005, the children of Virginia Primary School began to use the Circus as a green learning and growing space, and the following year, new iron railings filled the gaps to full heritage specifications courtesy of funds raised from the Ironmongers Company. Andy Willoughby, who continues to be integrally involved with the Friends as its valued gardener, was employed for half a day a week with volunteer support and a modest planting budget. The events continued over the years, and the green spaces literally blossomed. Funds for benches designed by Michael Marriott were raised in 2008, so the Circus became an area where people could sit and linger. In the same year, a comprehensive Conservation Strategy for Arnold Circus was produced, with the subsequent capital improvement works taking place in 2009.

Today, while capacity issues dictate that the Friends' activities are focussed less on events and fundraising, and more on keeping the bandstand safe, clean, and flourishing with flowers and biodiversity initiatives, the glorious fact remains that the founding vision has been achieved.

Right: Flyer designed by åbäke for the sharing picnic event, 2005

ARNOLD CİRCUS
SUMMER PİCNİC
SUNDAY 3 JULY 2005

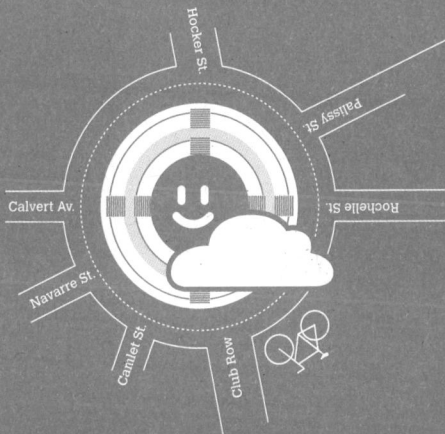

Friends of

Arnold Circus
+ Martino Gamper
+ åbäke

Hocker St.
Pallssy St.
Rochelle St.
Calvert Av.
Navarre St.
Camlet St.
Club Row

1–5 pm Sunday 3 July 2005
Arnold Circus, London E2

Bring your food and drinks,
and a dish to share.
We'll provide the lawn!

Mystery lucky draw
Free souvenir doormat
Wear your Sunday best!

For more information call Events
Co-Ordinator Alix McAlister 07985 713 458
or email arnoldcircus@gmail.com

Supported by:
Tower Hamlets Borough Council
Southern Housing Group
DMC Consulting

আরনল্ড চার্কাস আমার পিকনিক

২টা – ৫টা রুবিবার ,৩রা জুনাই ,০৫
আরনল্ড চার্কাস, ই ২

আপনার খাবার ও পানিয় সাথে আনবেন .
সম্ভব হলে আরও একমুঠা খাবার আনবেন.
আমরা বসার জামগার ব্যবস্থা করব.

লাকি ড্র
ফ্রি স্যুভেনির ডোরমেট
আপনার সুন্দর কাপড় পরে আসবেন .

Demand and Supply.
Martino Gamper, 2020

Necessity is the mother of many inventions, and this was the case back in 2005–06.

One of the many stories goes like this…

In the late 90's, when I first moved to London and frequented the area, Arnold Circus was abandoned by most locals. The bandstand and Circus were exclusively used by gangs and drug dealers and had become very unfriendly for most local residents. I was involved in organising various events and activities with åbäke and the Friends of Arnold Circus group, who congregated around my friend Leila's local café. Our aim was to help the Boundary Estate residents and other East Londoners safely use this beautiful, inner-city green island.

Our first intervention was a sort of sabotage renovation — we weren't supposed to touch the bandstand because it was listed, but it was so decrepit we had to do something. As we were not officially part of the Friends of Arnold Circus, some of us gathered one day to paint the bandstand without waiting for any authorisation. A few months later, we organised a sharing picnic. We covered the whole of the upper tier of the Circus with a green carpet (which was later used at our friends' wedding in Wales). Sitting

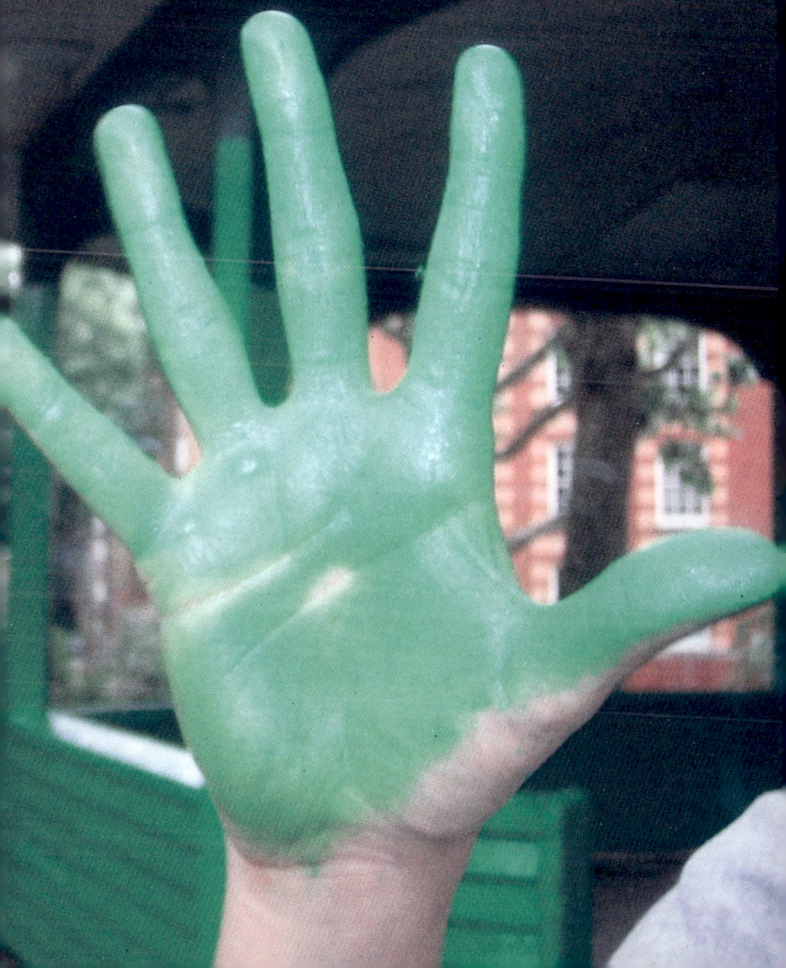

and sharing food around the floor, we soon realised that we'd like to elevate ourselves — a bit like when someone a few thousand years ago realised that sitting on a low stool or makeshift trunk was a more comfortable way of sharing a meal or working. The necessity was clear.

The idea was mooted by someone that we should buy chairs or stools from a well-known blue and yellow Swedish furniture brand.

"NO!" I said. "No way, not over my dead body will I go and drive 20 miles to the nearest outlet, and spend relatively little for not particularly permanent seating." I decided to create my own solution, since I'd graduated not long before as a furniture designer.

The brief was clear: a simple, versatile stool, easy and affordable to produce. But there are so many ways to design an elevated sitting object. First to decide on was the material, then the shape, then the production and, finally, it all had to sit within the Arnold Circus context.

Luckily, my friend and fellow graduate, Rainer Spehl had designed the successful Qoffee stool — a humongous version of a plastic coffee cup. It was designed as part of a student project at the Royal College of Art, but became widely used outside of that institution. It was produced in Somerset by Wydale

Plastics with a process called rotational moulding. This process is normally used to produce objects that predominately need to be hollow, large and/or complex in shape, for example, kayaks, water tanks and agricultural equipment, such as cattle feeder troughs. A plastic material, normally in powder form, is placed into a hollow mould, usually made from cast aluminium or sheet steel, which is then heated in an oven whilst rotating. The polymer gradually melts and 'lays-up' on the inside of the mould.

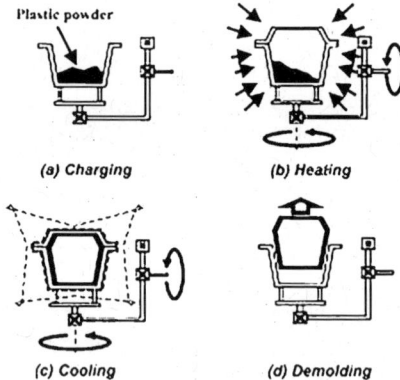

(a) Charging

(b) Heating

(c) Cooling

(d) Demolding

This technique was explored early on by Tom Dixon; he produced a range of 3D lighting objects. The most significant was the translucent coloured plastic 'Jack' light.

Right: Prototype marked-up with corrections. Three original cardboard mock-ups of the stools in the old Belsham Street work-life space, 2005.

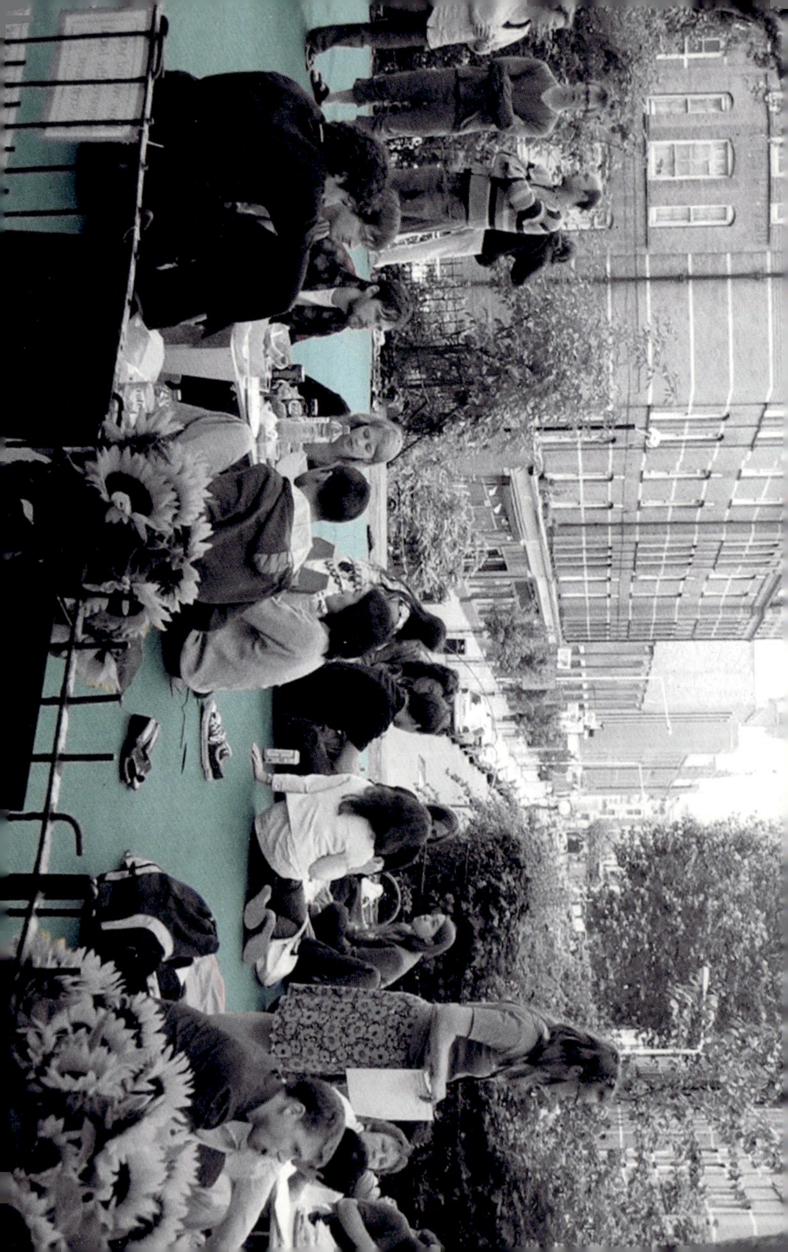

Left: The sharing picnic, 2005
Above: Carrom competition, 2007

Having been introduced by Rainer and Tom to this process and the manufacturer, my idea was to make a simpler, less expensive mould by folding sheet metal into a three-dimensional stool. This was first modelled in cardboard by my then intern, Hiroko-san. She made three beautiful looking 1:1 scale models that felt instantly right. The shape, being a mix between a tapered octagon extrusion and a corner (another obsession of mine), and the mix of the octagon bandstand from Arnold Circus and the corner seemed to make sense.

So, here we were: process found, producer found, shape done.

The only thing that was missing was the funding. Friends of Arnold Circus member, Anna Salaman had found a grant from Tower Hamlets Council that could be spent on local regeneration projects. But, since the funding wasn't quite enough to pay for the tooling, I added the other half towards that, and off we went.

The first delivery of stools arrived a month later, in three shades of green (green being the colour we had used to repaint the Arnold Circus bandstand). At the next sharing picnic, the stools were used for the first time — and they have been used ever since for all of its events.

Right: Kajsa and Maki being taught how to play Carrom by Liaquat (Squat), 2007

This is the first part of the story. The second part is how these stools got out into the world. It took a few years for me to realise that the stools could also be sold and become a commercial product. Leila McAlister from Leila's Shop told me that she kept fielding requests to buy the stools.

The prevailing design method is that following a brief from a company, one develops a product that fits within the company collection. That work would then be assessed to ascertain that it makes commercial sense. By doing a calculation balancing production cost and market perception, the hope is to create a need, so that it could then become a long-lasting and commercially viable product, paying small dividends to the designer. Supply and demand.

Somehow, this stool was developed the other way around. The need and context were obvious, and the discovery that they could be useful beyond this particular environment was unplanned, but apparent. I introduced new colours and sold these via a web shop. Later, I adjusted the shape and enlarged the seat size for comfort.

The stool has now been in production for 15 years, manufactured in three countries around the

Right: This wooden version was made with the help of Darryl Ward and his chainsaws and a big log of macrocarpa (Monterey cypress) in 2017. This stool-making by chainsaw has become a recurring event over the years; this first small wooden stool for Grey, pictured, was made as the prototype for the new smaller version called Arnoldino (see p.79). Thanks to Katie & Darryl for letting me use their porch.

world: in Somerset, UK; in New Zealand, in collaboration with my friend, the interior designer, Katie Lockhart; and in Australia by Anna Mackay.

The latest addition to the family is the smaller *Arnoldino*, born from a mini stool I'd carved in wood for Katie and Daryl's daughter, Grey in 2018. This stool seemed so cute that we decided to start production in New Zealand and, subsequently, the UK.

It always surprises me how many ways this hollow plastic container has been used. As a bucket, bin, baby bath, planter, laundry tub, turkey briner, ice bucket for a party, side table, makeshift toilet, plinth, chair base, large sangria punch bowl, helmet, toy container... and one New Zealander wore one as a Halloween costume.

After all these years of selling and shipping out boxes full of stools, my thanks go out to Momosan and Rosie, who have helped me run the UK logistics. The stools now fill many homes, gardens, galleries and cafes around the world.

Never would I have imagined that the humble little stool would corner the world.

Left: Old stools containing the plastic
pellets used to make new stools
at the production facility in New
Zealand, 2021.

Arnold
Alex Klein, 2019

In 2004, I was living in Shoreditch, at the corner of Great Eastern Street and Curtain Road. Although I had cheap rent and a spacious loft, the East End was at a tipping point. It would soon see an influx of the hipster bars and clubs that were an outgrowth of the galleries and restaurants already populating the Hoxton scene. This transition was evident in my ritual Sunday walks to the Columbia Road Flower Market that would often lead me deeper into Hackney and back home through Bethnal Green and Spitalfields. Crossing Kingsland Road, I would pass Arnold Circus, a small roundabout framed by brick housing units that encircled a somewhat shabby, elevated park with a gazebo at its centre. Aside from having an artist friend who resided in one of the modest flats in the complex, it seemed to me an otherwise unremarkable landmark that I encountered on my Sunday strolls and tried to avoid late at night. At the time, I was not aware that, like many corners in London, Arnold Circus had a more complex and layered history that echoed the changing landscape of the city itself. Constructed in the late 1890s as the Boundary Estate and home to the area's first public housing, it can be seen as emblematic of the city's diverse shifts in populations, economies, and purposes.

By the summer of 2005 I was starting to pack up my grad student life in preparation for a move to Los Angeles. Shortly before my departure, our friends from åbäke invited me and my partner, designer Mark Owens, to swing by a picnic they were helping to organize at Arnold Circus. I distinctly remember being surprised by the cheery atmosphere of this park that I had previously passed by so many dozens of times. I recall the poster for the event, and the familiar faces gathered together, games, food, good energy, and celebratory decorations. I also remember the bright green stools designed by Martino Gamper that dotted the scene. The fact that these stools were designed in 2006 is beside the point. In my memory and imagination, they are part and parcel of the re-energization of Arnold Circus.

Fast-forward to 2011 and another move, this time to Philadelphia to take a position as a curator at the Institute of Contemporary Art (ICA). The ICA's history is rich, but its building has the austerity of early 1990s postmodernism. Soon after my arrival I initiated a project, *Excursus*, with the aim of providing a space for people to come together and to make connections at the intersections of art, design, the archive, and conversation. Somewhat

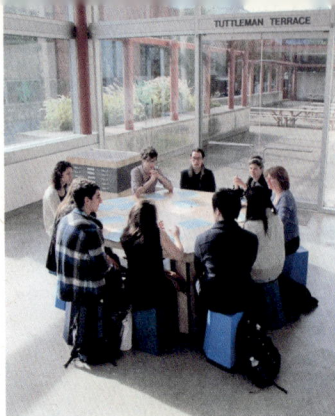

similar to Arnold Circus, this interstitial area of the building had been largely forgotten and was in the process of being reclaimed by the social. Working with artists, designers, and publishers, we aimed to create a flexible and inviting environment. Our first resident was Andy Beach's *Reference Library*, whose installation was themed around the former Philadelphia bookshop and radical press,

the Centaur (1921–42). By day, the bookshop was a respectable venue for the latest modernist literature, and by night, it was a hangout for local bohemians and a place to procure illicit booze during Prohibition. The logo for the Centaur was designed by the iconic American woodworker and printmaker Wharton Esherick. At the ICA we hung a neon version of Esherick's logo in the window so that it would be visible from the street, and we displayed one of his original Hammer Handle Chairs, whose structural elements were constructed entirely from off-the-shelf axe and hammer handles. Alongside these historical references and auratic objects, we included an array of Martino's Arnold Circus Stools.

The stools fit in perfectly with the intended flexibility and responsiveness of the project, which ranged from serious conversations about art and theory to an afternoon of playing chess, reading

books and perusing letters, a community Ribbon Bee, a performance, a book discussion, and many cups of tea. Soon, other museums that had seen the project at ICA also began to employ the stools in areas of their buildings that they were eager to animate and humanize. Once the first instalment of *Excursus* came to an end at ICA, the stools soon migrated to other parts of our building and started to take on other

uses. They first appeared as auxiliary seating for visitors in our lobby and for hosting guests over the occasional home-cooked meal. Martino even visited us from New Zealand on his way home in 2015 in order to join artist Peter Shire in conversation. But as time wore on, and as ICA staff changed, knowledge of the original purpose of the stools and who made them soon faded from institutional memory. Although the Arnold Circus Stools were still being used as extra seating for concerts and holiday parties, they also began to be incorporated into exhibitions as gallery furniture and as seating at computer stations. Since then, I have also seen them employed in the museum in a variety of creative and unpredictable ways: as a storage bin for unwieldy poster rolls, a temporary recycling container, an office side table, an umbrella holder, and as a place to rest tools during installation construction. Writing from 2019, it has now been eight years since the stools first travelled across the Atlantic to ICA. Although most people who encounter them don't know what they are, in their current home, disassociated from their status as precious design objects, the Arnold Circus Stools are truly freed to be multifunctional.

Right: The first version of the Arnold Circus Stool (ACS) bench outside our Tudor Road studio in Hackney, 2011

Egg
Michael Marriott, 2019

When I first met Martino, sometime in the late 1980s, he used to be a lot bigger all round. Mainly because he ate so much chocolate. His favourite was Easter eggs; he would get through at least one a day, from when they first arrived in the shops, until Easter — from then on, once they were reduced, he would stockpile them. They would typically be half-price within a week, so he'd quite quickly accumulate enough to see him through to the end of the summer. Springtime was like a harvest for him; he gathered those eggs like they were going out of fashion, from supermarkets, gas stations, corner shops, anywhere. Storing them became a project in itself. He became proficient in stacking them in particular ways, utilising the cardboard wrappers to structural effect and the corners of his room for extra support. Eventually, he turned to Blu Tack, which allowed him to tile whole walls with them.

I'm sure that his obsession with these egg-shaped chocolate shells was as much to do with how they were formed — their inherent seams and edges, their different inner and outer textures — as with the mysterious concave inner volume, holding not only cocoa-flavoured air, but also, more often than not, other chocolatey forms. It's undoubtedly no coincidence that both Easter eggs and his Arnold Circus Stools are made using essentially the same process. Martino would, of course, be drawn to rotationally moulding polyethylene as a means to realise his stool design, almost as surely as he could be spotted regularly cycling through Hackney, laden with exceptional quantities of Easter eggs.

Above: Young Michael Marriott sporting an Arnold Circus t-shirt designed for '100 cycle laps around the Circus', an annual event he came up with, which was happily adopted by the Friends of Arnold Circus.

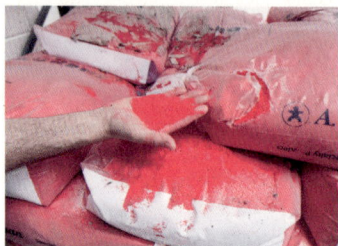

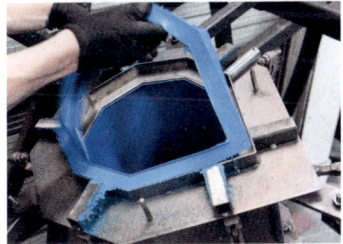

Rotational moulding process at
Wydale Plastics Ltd in Somerset.

Above: Each stool has to be carefully hand-finished with a special planer. The leftovers and shavings are re-ground and used for the black stool, which is made with 100% recycled material.

Right: Stone-like textures and shades can be achieved by mixing different powder colours.

Shop Till *You Drop*, 2012 at Hamburg Kunstverein. This special colour version, *ACS on Acid* was made as a swap to give to the contributors to this book. Each stool is a unique, one-off piece.

Jason Dodge & *Martino Gamper*
Exhibition at the American Academy
in Rome, 2013. Our show in the
Cryptoporticus used the ACS as
plinth and building block to create
seating and shelving.

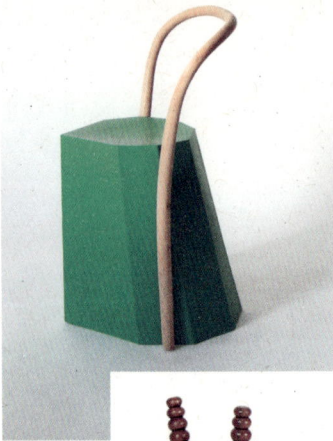

Above: Chair and desk for Max
James, 2010

Left: Various offspring of the Arnold
Circus Stool — I added backrests
to turn them into chairs and 'sitting
characters', 2011–16

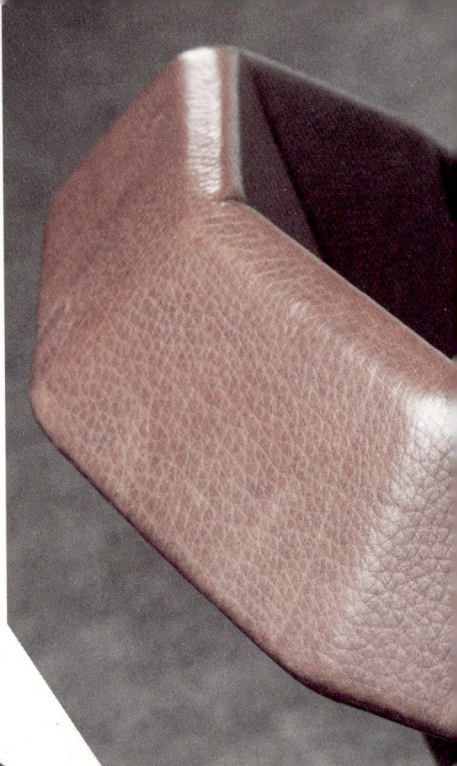

Leather version of the ACS, inspired by the folds and kinks of the stool. My intention was to create a leather chair without the usual subframe wrapped in foam and upholstery, but instead to stitch the structure into the leather skirt. This makes the backrest very light, and the folded collar helps to support the structure.

Wiktoria Stool, 2011. This shape was an attempt to make a softer, more feminine version of the ACS, but it had some serious design flaws when the first test moulding came back. We realised that we had managed to make a left and right version of the stool when moulding two stools together. This was going to be an impossible product to sell. Nevertheless, we have since used it as a convert mould for various projects. The moulds were used for the *Bench to Bench* project in Hackney Wick, as part of the Olympic legacy. The scattering of benches and stools form a trail from Victoria Park to the Olympic Park, leading people along the streets to make the route easier to navigate.

Two of East London's food temples using the stools for their outdoor seatings. This page: Leila's Shop on Arnold Circus, one of my favourite places to have eggs and tea. Right: Violet on Wilton Way with the flat white stool version

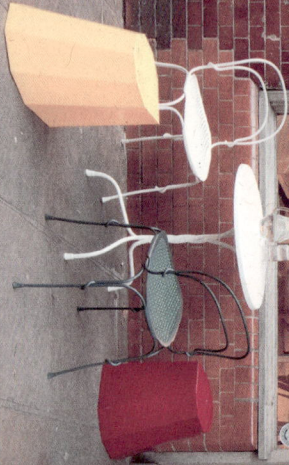

Above and left page: *Wiktoria Stools*, 2018. The *Wiktoria Stool* had a makeover. Tops were added to make the stool a little more fancy, but also more comfortable: the one on the left even got a new haircut and some colour. I made this one for *Chez Nina II*, Nilufar Gallery's pop-up club curated by India Mahavi during the 2019 Salone del Mobile. The idea of adding to and changing the initial object has always been part of my studio's way of working — the industrially produced stool was always conceived as a building material, a basis to create more varieties and spark new ideas.

Left: The fashion version in collaboration with Peter Pilotto's townhouse takeover for Brompton Design District, 2017.

Below: Linoleum-clad stool, 2017
Right: I made an Arnold Circus Stool
into a bathroom side stool, which
also functions as a clothes hook. This
was an idea that Charles de Lisle
had for a commission for Jessica &
Aaron's home in San Francisco.

Tabula Rasa, Museo del Risorgimento, Torino, 2017, in collaboration with Galleria Franco Noero.

I turned the ACS into a low table with old laminate kitchen tops from New Zealand, known as Paua Laminate. These stools were swapped with friends in New Zealand for either work or food (*polite notice Nova, I'm still waiting for that dinner*). Pictured here, the stool tables for Karl Fritsch, Kelvin Soh, Minna Pesonen and Nova Paul.

This stool was one of four versions I made for the epic collaborative show, *Gesamtkunsthandwerk* initially shown in New Plymouth, New Zealand in 2011. The show was a joint venture between Karl Fritsch, Francis Upritchard and I. These rough moulds were made with a local engineering company, but were lost when the rotational moulder moved warehouse.

Left: Stools for the Peter Pilotto and Christopher de Vos ready-to-wear runway show in the Palm Court at the Waldorf Hotel, London in 2018. This page: Peter Pilotto and Christopher de Vos AW 2017 runway show in collaboration with Francis Upritchard, Max Lamb, Bethan Laura Wood and Schmid McDonagh vintage dealers at the Waldorf Hotel, London.

Left: Momoko Mizutani on an ACS (*Please do not stand on the stool at home!*) and LPPL in an ACS.

Above: Exhibition design for publisher and designer, Christoph Keller's epic travelling show, *Beyond Kiosk — Modes of Multiplication*, 2009.

A Recent History of Writing and Drawing, Institute of Contemporary Arts, London, UK, 2008. The stool was used as part of the exhibition design.

The show, curated by Emily King, Alex Rich and Urs Lehni, was an interactive exhibition exploring the creative potential of graphic technologies. The ICA's lower gallery was transformed into a workspace, where a number of machines were developed to enable writing and drawing.

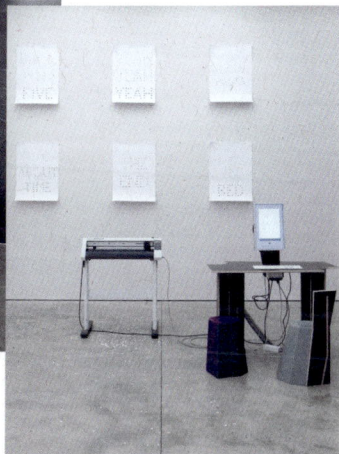

The British Art Show 8, 2015. ACS by the bookbinding table, which was used for workshops and bookbinding lessons in Leeds, Edinburgh, Norwich and Southampton. The title of the contribution was *Post Forma*. The project was driven by my interest in how an object can be transformed with public participation. I asked visitors to bring their belongings to be renewed rather than thrown away, then invited local craftspeople to host workshops in bookbinding, chair caning and weaving, and to share local traditions.

Post Forma was commissioned by the Yorkshire Festival and Hayward Touring, in partnership with the Yorkshire Sculpture Triangle and Arts Council England's Strategic Touring Fund.

ACS used to display a cupboard by Franco Albini as part of the *design is a state of mind* exhibition I curated at the Serpentine Sackler Gallery in London, UK; Pinacoteca Giovanni e Marella Agnelli, Torino, Italy; and Museion, Bolzano, Italy. The show featured an extensive display of shelving systems from the 1930s to the present day. These formed the backbone to organise and exhibit collections of objects from the personal archives of my friends and colleagues.

The Flight of the Dodo, Project Arts Centre, Dublin, 2008, curated by Jonathan Carroll and Tessa Giblin. The stools have custom backs and hold copies of Ryan Gander's book, *The Boy Who Always Looked Up*.

Stanze e Camere, Triennale di Milano, 2009. I made the ACS into a lamp using a stool and a concrete cast of the stool, in a direct homage to the Castiglione brothers' *Arco* lamp. Also pictured, stools with backrests used as chairs.

Condominium, Galleria Franco Noero,
Torino, 2011
At Casa Scaccabarozzi, also called
Palazzo Fetta di Polenta.

Arnoldino was born in 2018, after experiments in wood (see my chainsaw events on p. 31). It is a new, small addition to the family with even more uses: Champagne bucket, vase, planter, bin, circus stand for elephants...

Olivia & Vivi's first modelling job showing the potential uses of the new baby version.

Right: A bigger version of Grey.

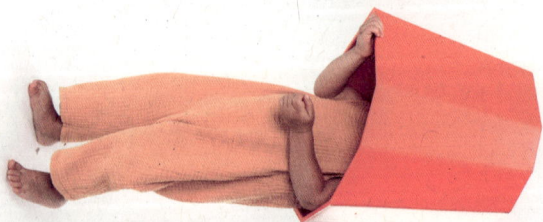

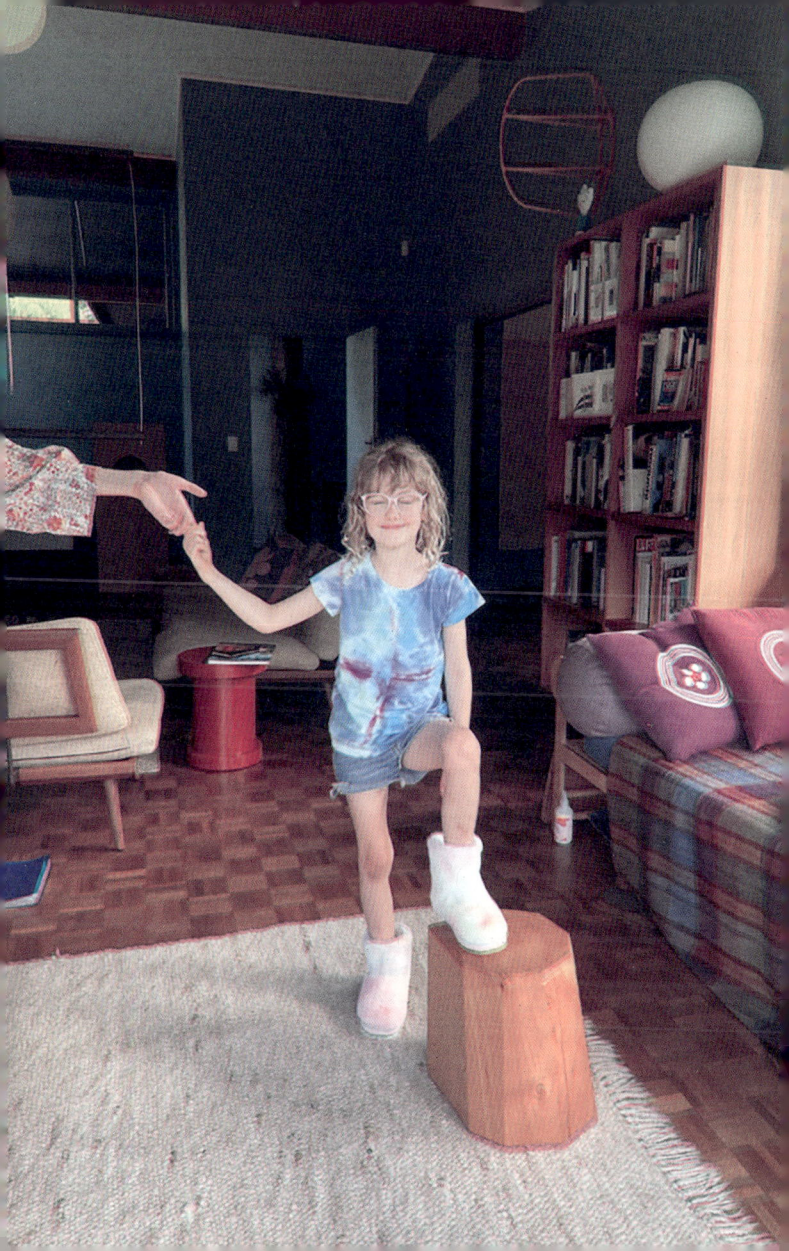

Café Le Look, Paris, 2008.
Interior design in collaboration
with Ludivine Billaud.

Keywords: Stool Guess Design Ripoff Nice Fibreglass Injection Moulding People Thought Plastic
A conversation between Martino Gamper and Rainer Spehl[1], 2019

Martino Gamper (M): How did the Qoffee cup project come about?

Rainer Spehl (R): It was when we went to the Tate, if you remember? All these bloody art students had to do a working stool — and no one followed the project. So, my idea was to do one of these coffee cups in plaster. It looked so beautiful that I sat down with Gabi and we both said, "hey, why don't we do this — bigger?" I worked up a model in plaster. That fine plaster was amazing, and when I cut open the cup, it was really very good looking. From there it was pretty simple.

M: Do you remember what made you do the plaster cast? Were you doing some project with what's-her-name in the ceramic department?

R: No, we were supposed to make a 1:5 model of something and this was more or less the size. I think we were playing.

M: Yes, as you do — you play, you think... Did you think of other shapes?

R: No. It was pretty much the first idea. I didn't feel like doing something complicated or technical — I was looking for one idea, one thing. The rotation moulding came afterwards. First, I made a big wooden one, which for a long time was in the åbäke studio.

M: Did you have any thoughts about what technique you might use — with the fibreglass?

R: It came quite quickly, because at the time Tom Dixon was doing his rotation moulding.

M: But I remember you working with a crazy fibreglass guy. What's his name? He poisoned himself with fibreglass, with polyester. Steven, I think. No, Pete. He was in the sculpture department.

R: Yes, but that was later. That was only for the degree show, because I had to make seven, eight, or ten — something like that.

M: So you made the wooden one first...

R: Yes, then I could use that to vacuum-form one stool for the show, to have a full-size mock-up. The fibreglass came much later when I had to reproduce them and make some for Ben Kelly, who designed the Hacienda.

M: Since then, you've been working with wood and on unique pieces. That's pretty much the opposite of plastic moulding. Why?

R: It's the other way round. I was always more into wood than plastic. It was just for the Qoffee cup — that was the material because a coffee cup is made of plastic. It fit the project. I mainly do wood, but it's not that I only do wood — I have worked with steel and brass, but you don't see it so much.

M: I think it was something you didn't necessarily plan to do. It was something you started, and you realised there was traction. You wanted to follow it up as well, because people were interested. At the time, it was something you could do without having a big workshop, given what you had available in London.

R: Yeah, and it was a super nice project to follow up, and to see that it can actually work — you can make it work without necessarily making something yourself. That was pretty good, and the first time I understood the 'designer' idea — you come up with an idea, you make it work, and then you move on to the next idea.

M: åbäke wrote a question for me, "How much of the Circus stool is a rip-off? Or an homage to the Qoffee stool?" I wouldn't see it as a rip-off. I think homage definitely, and influenced definitely by the manufacturing, by the rotation moulding and what they could make; what was available then in terms of money, possibility and the mould. I wanted to make a mould that was different, not an aluminium cast — the shape of the stool is the product of a bent sheet of metal.

R: Your stool is also pretty similar to what you did for the Tate, right? That alucobond stuff you did.

M: True — funny. I've always been a bit angular in a way. When I was a student in Vienna, I remember seeing that some designer had made one of those toy bones for dogs to chew on, which was made of facets. It was organic. It was 1994 and I thought wow, this is amazing. It was the first time I had seen an angular, faceted design. They'd taken an object and removed material to get to a shape. To cut a long story short, I was experimenting with laser cutting, which was pretty new then. The Circus Stool actually came out of the corner idea*. I'd always wanted to do a stool in solid wood.

R: Ah, ok.

M: Anyway, there was the bandstand with eight corners. I got back to this corner obsession I have. I was thinking, a steel mould, folded — it hadn't really been done before. Well, not so much — it had been done, but not as the ultimate shape. Usually, people welded bits together, round bits and square bits. I thought, I can do a very simple mould that doesn't cost much, by folding.

R: I remember, you were always interested in making a steel mould, and not a cast — more like a flat sheet that you can fold. You'd been fiddling around with it for some time.

M: Did you ever feel it was too close to yours as a project?

R: No, no. The amazing thing about rotation moulding — as I found out through Tom Dixon doing something — is that it's actually affordable for someone like me or you. I don't think it's a rip-off at all. You used the connection because the company was really good, and that's totally fine by me. It was kind of a silly question. It can't be a rip-off — it's totally different.

M: Yeah. I mean, it's a stool. At one point, I was amazed at how you could have a business with

Distant relatives: an Arnold Circus Stool and a *Qoffee Stool*

such a clever idea for something. I have to say, when you did it, I was like, "that's good". But obviously, I didn't start mine as a business. It started off as something for the Circus and then it slowly became a product.

R: When did you develop the Arnold Circus Stool?

M: 2005

R: That was a bit later, but not that late. It's taken on some similar production methods, but I wouldn't call it a rip-off at all.

M: You were really clever, in the sense that not many stools were made like that. In terms of being 'fit for process' you nailed it, because it was a cheap tool, you could change the colours very easily. You could stack them. They're durable. It has humour. If you try to remake that, in any other product, it could be very difficult. I'm sure you've been asked to, and I get asked as well.

R: Of course, I was thinking, "Okay... how can we do the next one?" Then it's very difficult. You don't want to start making a copy of something — that doesn't really work; trying to copy the idea, the success or the soul of the project. Maybe that's the connection to the wood, because I didn't see myself in the plastic world or product world as such, so I continued getting more into wood. I love how trees grow, it's such a brilliant resource, it looks amazing and you can do so many things. Ultimately, furniture was always made of wood.

M: Next question. They both became ubiquitous in art

centres in the world. Why? I guess they're pretty affordable, especially for education spaces.

R: Well, I think affordability is one thing. The colour, too, is very simple. You can create an interesting space with different stools, different colours. That's important for a lot of these places, that they have character.

M: It's informal seating in galleries, it's not like you want to sit in a big chair.

R: And they are stackable, easy to move, easy to take away, lightweight. The functional side is important for places like that.

M: You can use it as a stool, but equally, it's a bin.

R: Do people use your stool as a bin as well?

M: Yeah, people say, "Oh, I've been very naughty. I used your stool as a bin." I say, "It was designed as a bin." They get confused and they say, "What do you mean?" It's both, it contains — inside — and it supports — outside.

R: I can't think of many other stools in rotation moulding.

M: There are a couple of rip-offs of both of ours. I'm making them in New Zealand now and there was a contact from China, who wanted to do something in China, and asked me how I felt about it. I wasn't sure — they said they do injection moulding. That defeats the purpose a little bit, because I know you could make a much cheaper stool with injection moulding, but you would lose all the characteristics, because first of all, you'd have to have a rip outside rather than inside. You need a very expensive mould. The unit price comes down, but it's already pretty affordable. Changing the colour would become more difficult, there would be a problem with the wall thicknesses, and there's actually quite a lot of plastic in injection moulding compared to rotation moulding. You have deformation. You have to sell a lot, lot more to pay back the mould, which is probably 100,000 Euro or something, I don't know.

R: Yes, I looked into a mould for mine. At some point, there was a company in the Netherlands who wanted to make it bigger — buy the whole thing from me — and the mould in Indonesia was about US $100,000. That's a totally different game. You'd have to sell about 100,000 stools.

M: I'm sure some people could do it. Some people are probably doing it somewhere in the world, but it's a different product. Your stool as well, at one point, was very much used in coffee bars — art centres and coffee bars, and for informal, extra seating for restaurants or bars. They can't afford to have too many chairs, they need space, something they can easily take away. It's a kind of occasional seating, isn't it?

R: Informal occasional seating, yeah. Sounds good.

1: Rainer Spehl and Martino Gamper studied Design Products at the Royal College of Art between 1997 and 2000.
2: The Tate Project was a joint brief between the RCA and Tate Britain. The students were asked to design a functional stool to be used for talks and tours around the gallery.

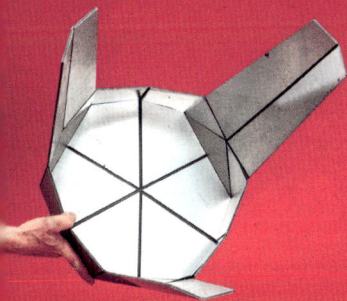

Me visiting the production facility,
Wydale Plastics Ltd. in Somerset in
2019

Thank you: åbäke, Adam Kershaw, Alan James, Albert Mairhofer, Alex Klein, Alex Rich, Alix McAlister, Andreas Schmid, Andy Willoughby, Angus Mill, Anton Kern, Anna Bosley, Anna Gamper, Anna Mackay, Anna Salaman, Anne Hardy, Alex Klein, Akiko Kobayashi, Andrew Hamilton, Andrew McDonagh, Benjamin Reichen, Bethan Laura Wood, Brad Watson, Charles de Lisle, Charlie Bones, Christopher de Vos, Christoph Keller, Cornelia Parker, Daniel Charny, Daniel Silver, Darryl Ward, Emily King, Erin Thompson, Finn Williams, Francesco Feltrin, Francis Upritchard, Franco Noero, Friends of Arnold Circus, Futoshi Miyagi, Gabi Klasmer, Gemma Holt, Grey Ward, Harry Thaler, Hayley Rawling, Henry Down, Hiroko Shiratori, Hiroshi Eguchi, Ian Veale, Ipek Altunmaral, Jason Dodge, Joe Cox, Jeremy Thomson, Jesse Beagley, Jessica and Aaron Sittig, Jochem Faudet, Joe Cox, Jonathan Carrol, Kajsa Ståhl, Karl Fritsch & Lisa Walker, Kate MacGarry, Katie Lockhart, Kelvin Soh, Kelly Amor, Kevin Shurvinton, Leila McAlister, Leila's Shop, Leo Mairhofer, Letizia Ragaglia, Linda Egger, Ludivine Billaud, Luna-san, Maddie Banwell, Maki Suzuki, Marco Rovacchi, Marcus Mustafa, Margaret Calvert, Mariah Nielson, Matylda Krzykowski, Max Eller, Max Frommeld, Max Lamb, Michael Marriott, Minna Pesonen, Momoko Mizutani, Muf Architects, Naseem Khan, Nina Yashar, Noddy Pilton, Nova Paul, Olivia & Vivi Barbosa, Patrick Lacey, Patrick Mairhofer, Paul Paul, Peter Pilotto, Peter Shire, Pierpaolo Falone, Rainer Spehl, Rich Young, Rio Kobayashi, Robin Hatton-Gore, Ron Arad, Rory Fitzgerald, Rosie Putler, Ryan Gander, Sam Boanas, Shashil Dayal, Studio Gamper, Tall Paul, Tessa Giblin, Tiago Almeida, Toby Webster, Tom Dixon, Tom Gottelier, Tower Hamlets, UPS and Fedex guys, Urs Lehni, Valerio Prete, Walter Thaler, Wan Cho, Wydale Plastics Ltd, Will Shannon, Yana Peel

Galleries: Anton Kern Gallery, Michael Lett, Galleria Franco Noero, Nilufar Gallery, The Modern Institute

Institutions: Leeds Art Gallery, Kunstverein Hamburg, Serpentine Gallery, The Govett Brewster Gallery, The Hepworth Wakefield, Triennale Milano, Yorkshire Sculpture Park, Museion, Bolzano, Italy and Pinacoteca Giovanni e Marella Agnelli, Torino

Resellers (at time of printing):
Analograum — DE
Anna Mackay — AUS
Aprikose — USA
A small Triangle — UK
ataW — JP
Coexistence — UK
Domestica — IT
Edition Populaire — CH
Everyday Needs — NZ
Hato — UK
Haus — UK
Hike — JP
Kobi & Teal — UK
Monocle Shop — IT
More & Co. — USA
NOW — JP
Paraphernalia — GR
Poly Octo — AUS
Post Poetics — SK
Sailors of Rye — UK
Supereditions — FR
Twentytwentyone — UK
Utrecht — JP
Villa Noailles — FR

Companies:
Breamfold Packaging Ltd,
Matrix Polymers, Rotational Plastics NZ,
Wydale Plastics Ltd

arnoldcircusstool.com
shop@martinogamper.com
for enquiries

Pistachio Green ACS 2019.
All profits from its sale go to charities including the Friends of Arnold Circus